Dear Young Leader

Thoughts Every Young Leader Should Know

Ken Taylor

Publishing

DEAR YOUNG LEADER
Thoughts Every Young Leaders Should Know

DEAR YOUNGTRADER

The ... Stupid Trend

Copyright © 2017 by Simon Taylor

All rights reserved.

In loving memory of:

Leatha Mae Henderson

You bought me my first suit with your J. C. Penny's credit card.
Your love always shined strong enough to overshadow the trials
and tribulations of life. The sacrifices you made for us we can
never repay. Rest in all the love you gave to others.

Rosie Mays

You were my Senior Advisor, my closest confidant and a best
friend. Your STRONG resounding voice of encouragement, to say
that I could do anything, was always loud enough to drown out
the small voice inside me that said I couldn't. From my first laptop
for college to the late-night chats, Thank You. It's clear my life
would not be the same without you.

Acknowledgements

The completion of this book could not have been possible without the support of a loving mother who when recognizing her son possessed certain skills always pushed but never shoved, encouraged but never glamorized, kept me grounded but never held be back and loved everyone she ever came in contact with but never made me feel any less loved than anyone else in the world. The hands, feet and tongue that now allow me to do so much for so many were formed, nurtured and personified in you before you even knew my name. You are now and always will be my first love.

Before there was Marvel, I believed in Superheroes because of you. You stayed when many men left. You were my first pastor, first physical trainer, first success coach and first person to show me the power of wisdom. You taught me real men don't challenge their sons where they are strong, they challenge them where they are weak.

The first prayer I can ever remember praying was asking God for a brother. Who knew the pesky little reporter that always seemed to get on my nerves, would turn into an answered prayer. You have always pushed me to levels I didn't know existed.

God, Dude you are just awesome. Your awesome ability to take the consequences of my mistakes and transform them into catalysts for success is proof within itself that you are God. Thank you for always looking beyond the damage of the consequences caused by mistakes and still finding enough value in me to repair and not throw me away.

Introduction

It was June 6th, the skies were as blue as I had ever seen them. Picnic tables were lined with barbeque chicken, potato salad and my aunt's world famous banana pudding. I can still see the rolling of the eyes hear the panting of little cousins anxious to get back to the volley ball game they were called away from in our back yard only to be forced to listen to their Aunt Sheila talk about their cousin Lil' Kenny. It was my graduation party; I had finally become a man.

> "You did more your Freshman year than I did in my entire four years of High School."

To this day I can hear those words so clearly. She said it jokingly to our closest friends and loved ones. And as they roared in congratulatory laugher and love, my heart began to fill with anxiety. It never really occurred to me how active I was in High School. I was always just me. It was always understood to push and be the best. It was always understood that I had parents the employed the principal that excellence was a mandate not an expectation.

They were the epitome of this themselves.

I can still feel my Dad shaking me violently. Almost yelling, in his strong tenor voice, he would say, "Kenny get up. Get ready for school." As he was circling back to make sure I was up and getting ready, he would kiss me on the forehead every morning before heading the local factory to work. My mom would often arrive, just after, from her third shift job at a local nursing home, finish getting my sister and I ready for school, stand with us outside at the bus stop and see us off to school.

As horrible as our mornings were, our afternoons were worse. Five out of five of our school days, after slaving away at to rise to the challenge of academic success, the big yellow school bus would come down our street, stop, open its double doors to my mother waiving to the driver and waiting to greet me with a hug and her standard, "I missed you. What did you learn today?" However, after jumping off of the bus from step to step and jumping into her arms; rather than going in the house to watch afterschool cartoons I was whisked away to a church service, choir rehearsal, to her job to visit many of the patients that "missed seeing Sheila's kids," to a hospital to visit someone sick, to take food to a grieving widow or countless other issues.

Ok, by now you're probably wondering what this has to do with Leadership? The answer, EVERYTHING!

Before my Dad began to pastor, before my mom owned a daycare and before they had the had an audience they were active. I'm not saying that I have all the answers, hold the keys to ensuring successful leaders or perfect in any way. But this is what I know for sure:

Leaders are constantly in motion. Whether they are following a path or mimicking an action, a follower must see an action to allow them to follow. I am the leader I am today because of the unyielding actions that I saw my parents have. The early mornings, the late nights and the trials that transformed into triumphs.

Leaders are wrong out front. Positive change can only come from authentic leadership. One of the worst mistakes a leader can make is to try to portray being right when they are wrong. That type of leadership is rooted in pride rather than effectiveness.

Leaders are confrontational. Leaders are always challenging the confines of normality. They are blazing new paths and testing the limits of innovation.

Leaders, as my father taught me, challenge their followers where they are weak, not where they are strong. Leaders jobs are to fortify and strengthen.

Leaders inspire leaders to become leaders that inspire other leaders. The fallacy of society is that we believe there can be only one leader. Many believe that only one person that is responsible for casting vision and leading that vision into execution.

Leadership is dynamic, it is hard, it is not for the faint of heart but above all else leadership is essential. Leaders are society's first responders in times of crisis and turmoil. They are the ones that are tasked with guiding us through tumultuous times and the ones we place our faith and trust in to guide us through those times. Leaders get credit for the victories and the blamed for defeats. Leaders are the burden bearers of our society.

It's my hope that these thoughts will encourage, uplift, challenge and fortify leaders of all ages as they navigate the burdens and experience the joys of leadership.

Dear Young Leader

◆

People may argue with you about your politics, and they may argue with you about your religion, but they can't argue with your results.

❧

When working to achieve greatness, excellence is not an option, but a mandate.

Dear Young Leader

❖

We are the things that we repeatedly do; therefore, excellence is not a single act, but a habit!

Many hands make light work.

Dear Young Leader

Learn to love others the way they want to be loved.

Perception is reality. Therefore, the power to change reality often lies with changing a mindset rather than changing a circumstance.

Dear Young Leader

Adversity is just a tool that reminds us of who we are as we overcome it.

Your gift will make room for you and cause you to stand in the presence of greatness. Your work ethic and character will determine how long you stay there!

Dear Young Leader

❖

When you feel like giving up, and when you think your enemies have won, gather yourself, take time to breathe, then declare to the world, "More weight!"

∞⟨⟨∞⟩⟩∞

You can't talk and listen at the same time. Shhhhh!

Dear Young Leader

You can't operate in your feelings and operate in excellence at the same time.

Watch your weight! Identify what weighs you down and trim down when necessary.

Dear Young Leader

The covert attempts of your enemies to destroy you will will result in your open triumph over their efforts.

To empower a community, you must empower its people.

Dear Young Leader

When others are not worthy, be graceful.
When they're wrong, be merciful. When
they are down, be their encouragement.
When they are lonely, be closer than any
brother. When they are in danger, be their
protector, and when they are afraid be their
comforter. Needs are always changing, but
no matter what the need is, always be the
one that can meet it.

Dear Young Leader

Let them see you falter, let them see you stumble, but NEVER LET THEM SEE YOU QUIT!

Celebrate the small wins as you do the big wins. A small win is always better than a big loss.

Dear Young Leader

Never take a "no" from someone that doesn't have the power to give you a "yes"!

Set your price high, not low, and wait. It may take longer, but at least you know the person who accepts will truly sees your value.

Dear Young Leader

Effective leaders are transparent but not judgmental, forgiving but not ignorant to malice, and, above all else, dedicated to pushing others to be the best person they can be.

Trustworthiness is the currency that fuels loyalty.

Dear Young Leader

Don't be afraid to make a severe withdrawal from others so that you can make room to make a significant deposit into your life.

Observe, assess, decide, act!

Dear Young Leader

The next time someone decides to tell you that Rome wasn't built in a day, kindly reply, "That may very well be true, but that's only because I wasn't the contractor." Don't allow others to confine you based on their own mediocrity and limitations.

Dear Young Leader

A change of action is not always a change of heart.

True vision is never accomplished, but is always expanding and evolving.

Effective leadership isn't just a catch phrase--it's a lifestyle.

The packaging is often more important than the product. The value of filet mignon is diminshed if it's served on a trash can lid.

Dear Young Leader

One of the reasons many people can't control their emotions is because they don't recognize how much power emotions actually have. Recognizing how much power emotions have is the first step to controlling them so that you have power over them and they don't have power over you!

Dear Young Leader

The mistakes and failures of your past will consistently eclipsed by the achievements of your present and future.

Wise generals seek not only to expose what the recruit can learn from the veteran but what the veteran can learn from the recruit.

Dear Young Leader

What do you call a debate with an uneducated, ignorant person? A waste of time! Iron sharpens iron, but everything else just makes it dull!

The ability to remain silent is a strength, not a weakness.

Dear Young Leader

The best way to gain power is to give it away.

Never confuse efforts with results.

Dear Young Leader

❖

Every moment you spend dwelling on your past is a moment you spend running from your future.

Always make more opportunites than you react to.

Dear Young Leader

The pain of letting go of the hurt of your past cannot be compared to the GLORY of grasping the destiny of your future.
#LetItGo

People can judge you, but only God can render the verdict.

Dear Young Leader

The will of a true warrior is never shaken, not because he doubts the abilities of his enemies or because he is unaware the skills that lie within them, but because he only focuses on and never, never doubts what lies within himself.

They will keep coming. You will keep fighting. You will win!

Trust is not essential to submission, but it sure makes it easier.

Dear Young Leader

You can't pursue penthouse dreams with a public housing mentality!

The moment you stop explaining yourself, you will need no explanation.

Dear Young Leader

The recipe for greatness isn't complex or found within confines of elaborate titles, beautiful red carpets, great fortune, or broad fame. It's found inside the heart of every person with a passion to serve their fellow man.

Many times the biggest barrier to finding the solution is thinking you already have it.

Dear Young Leader

Shortly after David slew Goliath, that he was appointed by Saul (the king) to be over the army. The Bible also says that he was accepted in his position. For many of us, the only thing standing between us being placed in position and JUSTIFIED in that promotion is the giant we refuse to slay.

Just because you may have the influence doesn't necessarily mean you have the power.

Dear Young Leader

The Highway to Divine Destiny often takes us down the detour of DIVINE DISCONNECTIONS!

If your heart is the center of your soul, then wisdom is the ribcage that protects it from the trauma of ignorance.

Dear Young Leader

Title-hungry people seek the title because they seek the weight of authority that the title carries, but the weight of authority comes with a weight of responsibility. That weight can only be carried after building your muscles through years of service!

Correction can only be received where there is respect.

Dear Young Leader

◆

When you have the vision to create, the courage to try, and the determination not to give up, you will have the grace to get it done.

Something of value only has value to those who value it.

Dear Young Leader

Not every person with a willing heart is an able vessel!

Presence does not determine access.

Dear Young Leader

At the moment that we think that we are above transgression is the moment we are closest to it.

There is a difference between leading and influencing.

Dear Young Leader

Never let your emotions speak louder than your plan.

Organizational culture isn't always the execution of the policies we execute but how the practice of those policies expose our true intent.

Dear Young Leader

Sometimes it takes affliction to activate Your anointing!!!

Good ideas are not limited to blue blazers and black suits.

Dear Young Leader

God will only make your enemies your footstool when he realizes that you are humble enough not to step on them, but to justify and raise them up!

Be careful not to pass off conscious decisions as consistent mistakes.

Dear Young Leader

The body cannot be effective with one leg constantly kicking the other and the hand always trying to pluck out the eye! A some point, each leg has to learn how to take its turn to move, and each part of the body must focus in on its specific assignment! Otherwise we become stagnant, bruised, and dismembered.

Dear Young Leader

Success may be just around the corner. but in order to get there, you have to CHANGE your direction! #Persevere

Real leaders are often transformed into vessels that can transcend others into their destiny.

Dear Young Leader

❖

You can not fully be who you were destined to be, until you recognize that you are not defined by where you are but who you are!

A hater is just another name for a person that can't tolerate your excellence.

Dear Young Leader

Don't let the pain you endured in the last season you experienced keep you from pursuing the joys in hidden in the next one!

Pain is a weight. Weight creates resistance. Resistance creates a tear. The body naturally fills in the void left as a result of the trauma with strength.

Dear Young Leader

The actions of the coward are never found among the courageous.

Pride can get you into some positions that you best talents can't get you out of.

Dear Young Leader

Real change is not a mindset but an action. A changed mind with no action to follow is nothing but a good mood. It may help you feel better about things, and even temporarily change your outlook, but when you look around, everything, in reality, is still the same!

Flying only comes when you disconnect from the ground, raise your altitude, and move faster than gravity can pull you down.

Dear Young Leader

True leadership is not determined by the amount of people that follow a person, but by the level of achievement they inspire others to reach!

Hate is an outward expression of inward insecurity, while love is an outward expression of inward strength.

Dear Young Leader

Not all kings come from nobility, succession, or great riches. Many have come from tumultuous situations, great misfortunes, and have been crowned on the heels of war. Moral: Some become king by receiving a crown, while others become kings by taking it!

They didn't call Superman what he was-- they called him what they identified him as. He was super and a man. What people call you is a reflection of how they perceive you to be.

Dear Young Leader

When challenged by frustrations of success, be careful to be frustrated with the situation and not your purpose.

Don't miss what is valuable by focusing on the deficiency .

Dear Young Leader

There is dignity and there is pride. Dignity will sustain you once you reach greatness, and pride will destroy you before you ever see it!

It's not a matter of 'do I always win? It's a matter of 'am I willing to do what it takes to win?'

Dear Young Leader

A leader that does not utilize the resources around him is like an amazing chef who refuses to use a knife. They will always start brilliant projects that they will never be able finish, the world will never have the ability to truly understand the magnitude of their gift, and their genius will always be overshadowed by a perception of incompetence.

Dear Young Leader

True authority always speaks to the heart of the
matter, while superficial authority skirts around it
like a child child trying to get around being caught
with his hand in the cookie jar!

Whatever comes out of you is a reflection of
what you put in.

Dear Young Leader

When you are in a state of mental stagnation, you can travel hundreds of miles and still be surrounded by what you were trying to leave at home. Progression has to do with the state of your mind and not the geographical state you are in!

Even geniuses once pooped on themselves.

Dear Young Leader

Kings and Queens act and look like Royalty. You will never see a Monarch on their throne in rags.

Some people would prefer being in bondage and wanted than free and rejected.

Dear Young Leader

❖

More often than not, a ridiculously awesome gift isn't enough to make people want to deal with a ridiculously nasty attitude.

◦◦◦

People will ask you who you are, but they will only believe the answer that comes from your actions.

Dear Young Leader

There often times can be a thin line between loyalty and self-destruction.

Just because you hit a homerun does not exempt you from running the bases. It doesn't matter how phenomenally well do you start the process, you still have to complete it!

Dear Young Leader

❖

Before every great exploit, there is a great trial.

━━━━━━ ✺ ━━━━━━

People are usually in your life for a reason, a season or a lifetime.

Dear Young Leader

True authoritative leadership demands respect by the presentation of a persons actions and character, not just because of their title. Know the difference? Do people respect you or your title?

It's hard to focus on who you actually are when you are so focused on what you are not.

Dear Young Leader

Fear is not acquired or an inherent trait--it must be taught.

Transition ends when the process is complete.

Dear Young Leader

Integrity is an inward evaluation of how you handle yourself, while reputation is an outward representation of how people see you. God only deals with your integrity, not your reputation.

The runway is just as important as the airplane.

Dear Young Leader

Before you can expect people to support your gift, you have to learn to produce. People cannot buy fruit that they can not see.

The condition of your heart often determines the condition of your life.

Dear Young Leader

Situations can change emotions, but emotions do not have the power to change your situation. Only your actions do! #DoSomething

In order to have a destiny you must have a destination. Purpose is nothing more than your roadmap to your destiny.

Dear Young Leader

One of the most essential traits of a king is the ability to discern the motives of his council.

Vision creates discipline. When you have a real vision you will protect it with your life, words and actions!

Dear Young Leader

◆

An essential element of leadership is surrounding yourself with like minds. Working with people who are not on your level will always cause frustration and can taint the purity of your name and integrity!

You are not meant to recover from some relationships, some arguments, and some frustrations. Sometimes they are meant to show exactly who a person is and that you should walk away.

Dear Young Leader

A distraction is ANYTHING that takes your focus away from what you should be focusing on! When your focus is tied to your destiny, a distraction becomes fatal!

Often, the presence of your pain will manifest itself as healing for others.

Dear Young Leader

For some, the only connection to greatness they will have is by trashing those who embody it. It's an unfortunate reality. So when dealing with those who are insecure, lazy, and would rather talk about those who do it rather than do it themselves, don't get mad--you just might be the closest to greatness they will ever get.

Dear Young Leader

Irrelevant people don't have haters, they have paranoia.

Never let your love for someone, in your pursuit of pushing them to their success, put you in a place where it can hinder or be a block to your own success.

Dear Young Leader

❖

Kings are never normal, and only normal people "fit in." Greatness always stands out!

Preparation converts instinct into quick calculation.

Dear Young Leader

When the shepherd starts speaking in a different voice, the sheep will ignore it and begin to follow anything that sounds familiar. In an environment where change is always constant, the consistency of the leader's voice is key.

Satisfaction is the root of mediocrity.

Dear Young Leader

To the pure all things are pure, and to the defiled all things are defiled. Watch when people consistently try to put a label on you--it's generally great insight to the type of character they possess themselves.

When you stop learning you stop growing.

Dear Young Leader

In the heart of the leader there can only be one of the following: a passion for greatness that drives the heart to contract and pump essential elements to the body to fuel this desire for excellence, or a contentedness in mediocrity that will never allow them to fully manifest their God-given potential. What's in your heart?

Dear Young Leader

A day not filled with challenges to overcome is a day not filled with the joy of victory.

Success speaks for itself.

66

Dear Young Leader

Everyone makes mistakes, but the key is to not allow your mistake to be a weight that hinders you from reaching success. Instead, let it be a catalyst that springs you to your destiny!

You can have a million strengths but if you aren't confident in them, they mean nothing. Confidence should always be your greatest asset.

Dear Young Leader

Your coach can train you, instill you the things that are needed for you to be successful, and give you the knowledge and techniques of a champion, but it's up to you to win the game!

Make sure your circle is always full of people whos words push you to your future rather than hold you in your past.

Dear Young Leader

❖

Often, the most complex problems in our lives are solved by simply going back to the basics.

Forgiveness is not synonmous with rememberance. Sometimes rememberance is the first step to ensuring you don't have to forgive the same event again.

Dear Young Leader

Be careful--the very person you thrown in the pit of insignificance now may hold the key to you survival later.

A clearly defined goal is not complete without a clearly defined plan to reach it.

Dear Young Leader

Your destiny does not have a responsibility to you; YOU have a responsibility to your destiny.

Always resend immediately, even if the response is that you will respond later.

Dear Young Leader

If you wish to be great, you must surround yourself with greatness. You must align yourself and your ambitions only with the things that embody the greatness you wish to become. Anything short of that will cause you to miss your destiny and fall into the bottomless pit of mediocrity.

You don't get points unless you shoot the shot, go for the touchdown, or step up to the plate and swing.

Dear Young Leader

Your past can only haunt you and affect your future when you still continue to deny its influence in your life. Those experiences can cripple you if you deny them, or empower you if you overcome them.

Setting goals based on your current level will keep you at that level. Setting higher goals will push you an even higher level of success.

Dear Young Leader

❖

You can't call yourself a shepherd with the mindset of a wolf!

⁓⁓⁓

Just like recovery and rest is an essential tool for muscle growth, you must also recover and rejuvenate your mind on your path to success.

Dear Young Leader

With great respect comes great responsibility. You can't demand respect without maintaining the responsibility that respect demands.

If you wait until you are completely ready to start, you will never start and never be ready.

Dear Young Leader

Impossibility is a myth that was created by those who simply were not bold enough to try.

Achieving the supernatural is impossible about without the natural. Always be proud of, but never become content with, the limitations of your humanity.

Dear Young Leader

Wise counselors often understand they must tell you the truth, even whent it hurts your feelings. They have the maturity to understand that temporary hurt feelings may be needed to push you to a permanent destiny.

The only substitution for hard work that leads to success is harder work.

❖

Growth is a product of change. Expecting to see growth without change is a product of insanity.

Being apologetic is an option for seeking forgiveness; however, change is a mandate.

Dear Young Leader

You will never see a true shepherd fat and his flock skinny and malnourished. A true leader will give all he can and survive on the essentials to ensure the physical and mental health of his flock.

Discipline is the only liberator when enslaved to the bad habits you seem unable to control.

Dear Young Leader

True transformation comes through education, by being taught that there is something better and transforming the mind with a commitment to apply the lessons you have been taught.

A weak person has the strength to say, "apology accepted", but it takes a mountain of strength to say, "I forgive."

Dear Young Leader

❖

The people you surround yourself with can often be a reflection of how others perceive you. If you consistently surround yourself with foolish people, then you probably shouldn't be offended if people mistake you for a fool! Birds of a feather... ah, you get the point!

Failing in a moment of weakness presents the opportunity for the recovery that makes us strong.

Dear Young Leader

Good things come to those who wait, but GREATNESS belongs to those who GO AFTER IT!

It's harder to truly appreciate the relationship you have with success if you have never had an encounter with defeat.

Dear Young Leader

❖

People don't attack people they believe are inferior. People only attack those they believe have the potential to be a threat. If you're being attacked, make sure you know your true worth because it's clear your enemies do!

⁕⁕⁕

A hard task ignored today will only be harder tomorrow.

Dear Young Leader

Excellence isn't a goal, it's a MINDSET!
What are you thinking?

Excuses have evil twins called explanations
and justifications. They never look like
accountability.

Dear Young Leader

Laugh out loud (no, really, out loud)! Then laugh until it hurts and cherish the moment. The power of laughter is always strong enough to remedy the pains of life.

Perfect opportunities don't repeat themselves to those who are imperfectly prepared.

Dear Young Leader

Your capability will often take you outside the realms of your comfortability! Step outside the box! You can handle it!

Curiosity kills cats; however, it makes leaders Great!

Dear Young Leader

Never confuse success with purpose. Success is man made, but purpose is God-given.

You can't date mediocrity and hope to marry success.

Dear Young Leader

A true advocate is one who no longer pleads the causes of another, but makes another's cause his own.

Two of the best motivators are success and failure. Use them both to your advantage.

Dear Young Leader

The moment you refuse to forgive, you are guilty of a greater offense than the one committed against you.

Success belongs to those who simply choose to keep going when everyone else chooses to let go.

Dear Young Leader

Some successes can't come with being good. Some require you to be great!

If you want something done, give it to someone that is truly busy!

Dear Young Leader

The challenges of today are merely seeds to be planted to cultivate tomorrow's harvest of success.

A hasty process will always produce a harmful result.

Dear Young Leader

If you're not making mistakes, you're not trying hard enough.

The harvest you produce is not based on what you want, but what you have planted.

Dear Young Leader

Doubt is the acknowledgement of the possibility of failure. You can't fail if you don't acknowledge that failure exists!

Never connect your identity to your service.

Dear Young Leader

People don't fight change they don't fear!

True visionaries will often find themselves waiting for culture to catch up with their innovation.

Dear Young Leader

◆

What you do will always prove what you believe!

❧⸙❦⸙❧

The quality of your success will not exceed the quality of your work ethic.

Dear Young Leader

Even fairy tales have their challenges!

Lies always come with consequences.

Dear Young Leader

Never confuse growth with purpose. Even weeds can grow under the right conditions. Check your roots!

Don't confuse the pit stop with your final destination. The purpose is for some things to change, not for you to stay.

Dear Young Leader

Sometimes you have to look at who a person is and what their actions constantly produce, and keep your distance. If they are consistently in strife with their spouse, their family, and everyone else then understand that eventually that conflict will extend to you. Love them, support them from a distance, and follow peace!

Dear Young Leader

◆

The strength of fear is limited, but the power of courage is infinite!

❧～✦～❧

You have to think bigger than your situation to find your way out.

Dear Young Leader

The quickest way to go crazy is to consistently try to make sure everyone else stays sane!

The biggest threat to success is comfort.

Dear Young Leader

❖

Never let anyone manipulate your mind. The manipulation of your mind equates to the manipulation of your life, and allowing someone to manipulate your life is the beginning of death.

Real leaders are confrontational. They will confront the weakness to pull out the strength.

Dear Young Leader

The hardest part of needing to let something go is getting past the fact that you want to keep holding on.

Love is unconditional, but relationship isn't.

Dear Young Leader

◆

Requiring obedience without understanding provides only for a change of method; however, obedience with understanding offers an environment that fosters perpetual growth! Leaders teach, not instruct!

The creation cannot give purpose to the creation--only the creator can.

Dear Young Leader

❖

The transition from simply dreaming to putting your dreams in action is when you transition from a mindset of hope to EXPECTATION!

Just because it's not fully time for a harvest doesn't mean you should't still see the buddings of fruit.

Dear Young Leader

Who made it to the finish line first, the tortoise or the hare? No one cares--they both made it!

FUTURE > FOOLISHNESS

Dear Young Leader

A wise man may ask a fool for his opinion,
but he will never ask a fool for his advice.

If it's not written, it doesn't exist.

Dear Young Leader

Interpretation is the most essential and detrimental part of any conversation or correspondence. It is amazing to think that a fool can be faced with insurmountable wisdom and they will still interpret the wisdom as foolishness.

Be careful with associations. You may not always share their actions, but you may find yourself sharing their pain, shame and consequences.

Dear Young Leader

Never let your own personal bias affect your ability to assess the credibility of your own argument.

You can only have faith in things that you trust.

Dear Young Leader

The selectivity of your "no" will often determine the quality of your "yes"!

Maturity isn't solely based on how your fight your enemies, but often how you handle them after you have won.

Dear Young Leader

Your struggle will reveal your weaknesses, but your weaknesses reveal your opportunities for growth!

It is never dishonorable to someone else when you choose to honor yourself.

Dear Young Leader

❖

Be intelligent enough to admit that you have weaknesses, but be wise enough to know to whom to admit your weaknesses.

Be intelligent enough to know to whom to admit your weaknesses.

The unit of measurement to determine the success of leadership is impact, not numbers.

Dear Young Leader

Preceding every great success are great failures! Failing isn't the problem--it's when you focus on your failure and let it keep you from moving on down the road to success that you transition from failure to defeat.

Don't focus so much on trying to make tomorrow happen that you neglect the responsibilities of today.

Dear Young Leader

A person's problems and challenges are directly proportionate to their influence and destiny. Billionaires don't have $5 problems!

Perseverance is often the key that transforms your life from a state of surviving to thriving.

Dear Young Leader

Success is an external manifestation of an internal resolve! Get your mind right!

Just because you have the tools and ability to win the battle doesn't always mean you should fight the battle.

Dear Young Leader

You may win some, and you may lose some, but you benefit from all.

Happiness and peace are an essential part of identifying success. If there is no happiness and no peace, then it's not success.

Dear Young Leader

Strength is the ability to hold on in spite of incredible challenges, courage is letting go when everything in you tells you to hold on, and wisdom is the ability to know the difference!

There is a difference between joy and happiness. Happiness often occurs because of situations, while joy will remain inspite of them.

The first step to gaining strength is authenticity. You must honestly evaluate your weaknesses. Only out of an authentic weakness can you gain genuine strength.

People are not afraid of heights; they are afraid of falling. Inspire confidence in one's ability to fly, and the fear is gone.

Dear Young Leader

100% of the time it's the fool who thinks they are the smartest person in the room. You can always spot them because they are usually talking the loudest.

Only after you have experienced defeat can you fully appreciate victory.

Dear Young Leader

Your purpose weighs more than your mistakes. Let purpose serve as your anchor, rather than letting others try to anchor you in the pitfalls of your past.

Mimic greatness so much that it becomes authenticity.

Dear Young Leader

When you wait on others to present an opportunity to you, you are enslaved by them. When you make your own opportunities, you are liberated by them. Assess, plan & execute!

The star of the show is often the first and last person on the call sheet.

Dear Young Leader

Sometimes it's the fall that infuses you with
exactly what you need to stand tall.
#DustYaSelfOff #LearnFromIt

Decisions are made by the poeople who
show up.

Dear Young Leader

I'd rather be seen as a failure after striving for perfection than to be successful at doing nothing at all!

Honoring the past doesn't mean perpetuating it.

Dear Young Leader

◆

There is a difference between influence and power. People have the ability to influence your success by presenting hindrances, but they do not have the power to restrict your access to it. They have sovereignty over their influence, but only YOU decide how much power they have over you!

The first step after an earthquake isn't assesing the damage, it's preparing for the aftershock.

Dear Young Leader

One thought that tells you that you can will always be heavier than a million circumstances that lead you believe that you can't.

Focusing on fear constricts and contaminates confidence.

Dear Young Leader

You will never be able to find freedom in the midst of bondage. Even bondage can seem to have its glimpses of freedom, but NEVER glorify those small benefits of bondage to escape the work it takes to be free!

Peace is the absence of the storm, while perfect peace is when you have peace inspite of it.

Dear Young Leader

There are some battles the wisest generals will lose and there are some battles even the foolish are destined to win. But while the fool celebrates his victory, the wise will learn from his loss and prepare for the next battle. To this end, the wise cements his victory over the war, and the fool's victory will be short lived, but the consequences of his surrender will last forever.

Dear Young Leader

Incredible challenges bring incredible opportunities, which bring incredible rewards!

Opinions should often change when challenged, but values and principles shouldn't.

Dear Young Leader

Just face the facts: You just don't have what it takes…to quit!

Leaves appear, disappear, change color, and bend based on the seasons; however, the roots always remain the same.

Dear Young Leader

In life, you learn sometimes people just won't like you. That doesn't mean there's anything wrong with you, and sometimes it doesn't make them a bad person. Sometimes people are just human. But for every one person who doesn't like you, there will be an army of people who do!

It's always easier to divide a group than it is to bring them together.

Dear Young Leader

Real fathers don't challenge their sons where they are strong, they challenge them where they are weak. True sons see the challenge as an opportunity for growth, rather than an excuse to escape the difficulty, pain and frustration of growth. Too many times we allow our emotions to define the challenge presented by our fathers as an attack from an enemy rather than from a loved one who is trying to prepare us for the real enemy they know is coming!

Dear Young Leader

❖

If you're not shining, you're being consumed by the dark! It's that simple.

~∞~

Build something with your life that will live long after you don't.

Dear Young Leader

❖

Many people spend an entire week, month, year or lifetime trying to convince themselves that they can, should and are capable of doing something. Funny thing is, it usually takes half that time, stress and energy to actually get it done.

People may not believe in you, but they have no choice but to believe in your results.

Dear Young Leader

◆

To some, drama and tension can be like a drug. When they are separate from it, they start to go through withdrawals and will do (or start) anything for a hit. Don't be their pusher.

Weakness is often the only path that leads to strength.

Dear Young Leader

❖

Passion is the currency that buys happiness!

Y❦∼

You may have all the vehicles necessary for you to reach your desintation; but it is still up to you to steer.

Dear Young Leader

Some people would rather perfect mediocrity than strive for imperfect greatness. Be great! It's in you!

Making sure that you prepare for all possible outcomes is the only mechanism that can guarantee victory.

Dear Young Leader

You can't change how your past has affected your present, but you have control over how your present will affect your future.

The worst thing you can do to reach success is weigh your strengths heavier than you weigh your weaknesses.

Sometimes you have to make a present sacrifice to have a future abundance.

Not every road that is fit to travel leads to your destination.

Dear Young Leader

Live the life NOW that will allow you to live the life you want to live LATER.

The wisest generals can often win the battle without engaging in a fight.

Dear Young Leader

Never misrepresent your intelligence by displaying the acts of the foolish. People believe what they see!

Laziness will always lead to destruction, while persistence and consistency will always lead to survival.

Dear Young Leader

❖

Maturity is having the strength to say what needs to be said, the intelligence to know that everything that needs to be said doesn't necessarily need to be said by you, and the wisdom to know the difference!

~ ೧ ೪ ೧ ~

The confusion of those you lead is not often a testament of their ignorance but an indication of your inability to improperly communicate.

Dear Young Leader

The first time, you can call it a mistake. The second time, you can say, "I'm still learning. It's a process." The third time, it's a habit that it's time to break!

Real talk about real issues gets you real results!

Dear Young Leader

Every day, every hour, every minute, every second you are selling your time. Time is expensive, and, much like goods, once you have released your possession of it to another entity, it's gone. Only you can decide the value of your time. Only you can decide what it's worth. The moment you decide your time is far more expensive than drama, frustration, and malicious people can afford is the moment you begin to live a prosperous life!

Dear Young Leader

People make mistakes. They do bad things and at times make the wrong decision. It's our nature. If someone hurts you and apologizes, owns it, and ceases the behavior, move past it and let it--or them--go. Living in constant irrational fear of them committing the same offense only inhibits you from living a stress-free life. Let it go or let them go.

Successful leaders don't work to build an environment where they are constantly needed. They work to build one where they are not.

Dear Young Leader

Love is a trial and your actions are the evidence. If you were on trial would your actions be enough to convict beyond a reasonable doubt or would you not make it past the grand jury? Love is synonymous with action!

Success often requires you to become the person no one thinks you are capable of becoming.

Dear Young Leader

The only thing worse than tapping out is not knowing when it's time to tap out. After a while, if you see you're losing the fight and you keep engaging, the other person isn't hurting you--you begin hurting yourself.

Opposition is the seed that produces the harvest of opportuntity.

Dear Young Leader

Leading with integrity means that often times you may find yourself being wrong upfront. Strong leaders use it to teach others, while weak leaders hide it because they would rather have the perception of strength than engaging the process it takes to actually cultivate it.

Dear Young Leader

❖

I never learned my body could heal from a scrape until I took the training wheels off of my bike.

⁓⁓⁓⁓⁓

Never judge a person's future by how they look in the present. The Ugly Duckling became a swan, and the most beautiful rose became dry and wilted.

Dear Young Leader

Figuring out what you want and who you want to be in life isn't hard. What is hard, usually, is determining what you're willing to give up in order to get what you want in life and be who you want to be.

There are two types of leaders: those who see achieving the impossible as the finish line and those who see it as the starting point.

Dear Young Leader

You can't use the same stone you used to beat someone over the head with to build them up! Build, don't bash!

The more you learn to love your job, the less it feels like work.

Dear Young Leader

Learning to fail is just as important as learning how to succeed. Because if you are in a situation where winning is infeasible and you handle it poorly, you can ruin future chances of success! Learning how to lose the best way to prepare yourself for a future win.

Dear Young Leader

If you let them, 5 little words can change your life and inspire you to achieve happiness you never thought was possible "I deserve better than this!"

Don't get so used to the slow pace of going up the mountain that you don't prepare for the speed on the way down.

Dear Young Leader

The absence of fear and wisdom will always lead to destruction!

Success is heavy, not light. You have to build an endurance; otherwise, you will crumble under the weight of your own success.

Dear Young Leader

Even with the purest of intentions, today's decisions can produce tomorrow's consequences. Regardless of how right it may seem, wrong seeds can never grow a right harvest!

Joy is infectious and can spread when you are exposed to it. Unfortunately, so is misery.

Dear Young Leader

Truth has the power to hurt; however, that should never be eclipsed by the exponential power it has to heal.

The absence of dedication will always lead to the presence of defeat.

Dear Young Leader

You should always be grinding and growing. If you're all grind and no growth it's time to reevaluate.

You value may consistently vary in other people's eyes, but it should always be the same in yours.

Dear Young Leader

Its impossible to find permanent satisfaction in a temporary place.

Experience may not always be the best teacher, but it can definitely be the cruelest.

Dear Young Leader

You weren't created to color in the lines.
You were created to redefine them.

Learn to control your fears and your fear
will never control you!

Dear Young Leader

Every big idea you have started with a small step. The fulfillment of every big idea that you have starts with a small step.

Who you are is who you were meant to be.

Dear Young Leader

Success promotes itself.

Faith has the power to move mountains, but you still have exert force. PUSH!

Dear Young Leader

You're only out of options when you stop looking for them.

Execution is to strategy as wheels are to a car. To be effective you need them both.

Dear Young Leader

Sometimes the best measurement of success is not what you have but but you don't have: Stress. Worries. Frustration.

Discipline is the backbone of determintation.

Dear Young Leader

Nothing can be birthed without some level of pain.

Good leaders exceed standards, but great leaders set them!

Dear Young Leader

Life does not play tricks on you, your mind does.

Discipline is the bridge between strategy and execution.

Dear Young Leader

The test doesn't come to kill you it comes to credential you for the next level.

When taking over a new position, never try to fill the shoes of the person before you. Nine times out of 10, they won't fit.

Dear Young Leader

Work hard everyday to be right about how wrong they are about you!

One person with a plan is the equivalent to a thousand people with a single idea.

Dear Young Leader

Discipline is having the strength and the wisdom to do what you need to do before you are forced to do it.

Fools are recognized by their voice, while the wise are recognized by their actions.

Dear Young Leader

Forgive yourself even when others don't
forgive you.

Stress comes from focusing on what you
think things should be, but peace comes
from learning to manage things as they are.

Dear Young Leader

A seed can only blossom where it is planted!

The determination of an idea being purely genius or purely insane is often its measure of success.

Dear Young Leader

Its hard to focus on who you actually are when you are so focused on what you are not.

***

Controlling others is easy, but controlling yourself is hard.

Dear Young Leader

The hardest part is convincing yourself; the easy part is actually doing it.

Speaking softly is often a better strategy to ensure being heard than speaking loudly.

Dear Young Leader

A train going through a dark tunnel is still on track! Keep going!

You will never be content with who you are focusing on what you do not have.

Dear Young Leader

As they mature, true leaders become less concerned with ensuring they have the biggest plate and become more passionate about ensuring everyone has something to eat.

Your attitude is often determines the difference between things being perceived as complex or chaotic.

Dear Young Leader

You don't excel despite your issues--you do because of them.

Stop focusing so much on making the right decision. Make the decision, and then do whatever it takes to make that decision the RIGHT one.

Dear Young Leader

The more you become obsessed with success and greatness, the less you worry about the opinions of haters and more about the words of those who are already great.

It's impossible to defeat someone who refuses to give up.

Dear Young Leader

Never start anything you can't sustain.

You may lose many battles, but remain undefeated.

Dear Young Leader

❖

There is no mixture of confidence and fear. It's one or the other. Pick your poison or pick your future.

∽◦❧∾

Resistance applied against propulsion (moving forward) is the force that is required to produce the lift. Both propulsion and resistance are needed to fly.

You can't control timing, and you can't control luck, but you can control you.

The prize of fighting fear is courage.

Dear Young Leader

There is a difference between purpose and dreams! When you forsake your purpose to pursue your dreams, you lose sight of who you are versus who you were meant to be!

Stability is the art of learning to triumph over the trauma of transition.

Immaturity is the state of being too young to know or understand what's right or what's best for you. Foolishness is knowing what's right and knowing what's best and choosing to do the opposite anyway.

Dear Young Leader

A foolish man surrounds himself with people that he has gained more than to gain the perception of wealth. A wise man surrounds himself with those who have gained more than him, knowing that they will have the ability to increase his wealth.

Dear Young Leader

Never ask for anything less than you need.

Defeat derives from a temporary situation
that has the ability to change to victory,
failure derives from mindset that must
change to produce success.

Dear Young Leader

❖

If their first answer isn't no, you probably didn't ask big enough.

∽⌇⌇∽

Emotions are synonymous with humanity. You should be cognizant of it, but never limited by it.

Dear Young Leader

Excellence always takes longer than mediocrity.

Always assume positive intent in others, but always prepare as if they have the worst.

Dear Young Leader

❖

Your brain's job is to create ideas, not to manage them. GET THEM ON PAPER.

Successful leaders don't strive to just have their followers be compliant. They strive to have them be committed.

Dear Young Leader

There are some things only isolation can produce. I've never seen a caterpillar go into a cocoon with friends and come out a butterfly.

Seasons don't change. They transition.

Dear Young Leader

A house of lies will always collapse under the weight of the truth.

If you want to be successful in every area of your life, find a mentor for every area of your life.

Dear Young Leader

The consequences of a lie will always be worse than the consequences of the truth.

If you apply enough force anything will eventually break. If you feel like you're trying and you can't break through, JUST KEEP PUSHING

Dear Young Leader

In the midst of unspeakable joy and heart-stopping pain, on this you can rest assured: the sun will still rise the next morning and still set the next evening.

Don't let a little success lead you down the path of a big failure.

Dear Young Leader

Don't Wait! Do it now!

It can take years to build credibility and one moment of impropriety to destroy it.

Dear Young Leader

A fool will remain a fool as long as he rejects the counsel of the wise.

A change of the mind changes consciousness, while a change of the heart changes the actions.

Dear Young Leader

After the announcement, everyone knows, everyone is aware, and everyone EXPECTS!

Dear Young Leader

◆

Sometimes the goal isn't reaching the stop of the stairs. Sometimes it is just taking the first step.

Dear Young Leader

Good leaders always lead with love and
follow with accountability.

Dear Young Leader

You can't act like a child and expect adult results.

Dear Young Leader

As a leader, if you have the privilege of being first, then you also have the responsibility for ensuring the successful passage of the last.

Dear Young Leader

❖

The state of our feelings often differ from
the state of our situation.

Dear Young Leader

❖

Dear Young Leader,

You have everything inside of you that you need to be successful. There is no force strong enough to stop you from reaching success and manifesting your destiny.

Confidently go into the future knowing you are fully equipped for the task.

Define your win, develop a path to victory and execute it with excellence.

Be Bold, Be Brave and Always Be You.